Jesting Angels

Jesting Angels

GOD'S LIGHTER SIDE

Ken Bazyn

RESOURCE *Publications* • Eugene, Oregon

JESTING ANGELS
God's Lighter Side

Resource Publications
An Imprint of Wipf and Stock Publishers
199 W. 8th Ave., Suite 3
Eugene, OR 97401

www.wipfandstock.com

ISBN 13: 978-1-4982-2057-6

Manufactured in the U.S.A. 06/01/2015

Contents

Preface

Proof Positive

If the proof is in the pudding,
whose sticky fingers will fetch it out?

Acknowledgments

ONCE AGAIN I OWE a special debt of gratitude to my wife, Barbara, whose love for poetry has rekindled my own, and to David Reynolds, who has raised important questions concerning style and meaning to improve my overall contribution.

Thanks also belong to Wipf & Stock for their willingness to offer yet another title to their ongoing line of first-rate Christian poetry and to Ian Creeger for his obvious typesetting craftsmanship.

Finally, deep appreciation is due to everyone who has helped to lift this fellow believer out of the downward pull of taking himself and his faith far too seriously.

The following publications deserve credit for first releasing these poems:

"I wish I were a soap bubble" in *World of Poetry Anthology*

"The Iowa State Fair" in *Cresset*

"Art Thou the One?" in *Duck Soup*

Introduction

Laughing Your Way to Heaven

"IF YOU WANT TO make God laugh," goes a joke by filmmaker Woody Allen, "tell him your plans."[1] Tomorrow does seem to have a mind of its own. What did you want to be when you grew up? And what are you doing today? Life's twists and turns have a way of overturning our expectations. When I was eleven or twelve, I became excited about the idea of becoming an architect—to make daring designs from the ground up. But I never realized how many skills you had to master: pouring cement, working with wood, brick-building, electrical wiring, heating and plumbing, and so forth. Then, having enrolled in a vocational agriculture class in high school, I was required to draw blueprints for several shop projects. I had the devil of a time gazing out at a three-dimensional world, then trying to reduce it to two on paper. The principles of perspective, well-known since the Renaissance, didn't seem all that natural to me. Later, when our high school class took a series of aptitude tests, wouldn't you know it, my score in spatial reasoning turned out to be below average. My career in architecture abruptly ended, since I obviously had no talent for it. Apparently God's favorite teaching technique is trial-and-error.

Of all animals, Aristotle once observed, only man is capable of laughter.[2] Indeed, there are three prominent theories that explain our human propensity for humor: one which emphasizes the release of tension, another that stresses the humorist's feeling of superiority, and a third which highlights a shift in cognitive perspective.[3] Freud thought humor a healthy defense mechanism that contributes to our overall mental health. Hobbes

---

1. Cooper, "Humour," 63.

2. Aristotle, "Parts of Animals," 1049.

3. Martin, "Humor," 540

called laughter a "sudden glory,"[4] in which we feel superior to those around us or to our own previous self. Schopenhauer believed laughter to be an immediate reaction to some incongruity just noticed. Think of the delighted surprise from that simple childhood toy, the jack-in-the-box, writes philosopher Henri Bergson: "As children we have all played with the little man who springs out of his box. You squeeze him flat, he jumps up again. Push him lower, and he shoots up still higher. Crush him down beneath the lid, and often he will send everything flying."[5]

So, of course, you'll find humor in the Bible. Witticisms, for example, punctuate the Old Testament's wisdom literature: "Like somebody who takes a passing dog by the ears is one who meddles in the quarrel of another" (Prov. 26:17). "Like a gold ring in a pig's snout is a beautiful woman without good sense" (Prov. 11:22). "It is better to live in a corner of the housetop than in a house shared with a contentious wife" (Prov. 25:24). "Dead flies make the perfumer's ointment give off a foul odor" (Eccl. 10:1). "But a stupid person will get understanding, when a wild ass is born human" (Job 11:12). In the final chapters of the Book of Job, a voice from a whirlwind clarifies how laughable it is to compare human intelligence to God's. Job is drolly interrogated as to whether he might catch the Leviathan with a fishhook or hang a rope through its nose; can he play with it like a bird or put it on a leash (Job 41:1–5)?[6]

On occasion, Jesus also resorted to preposterous (what G.K. Chesterton calls "gigantesque"[7]) images to convey his teachings. "[I]t is easier for a camel to go through the eye of a needle than for someone who is rich to enter the kingdom of God" (Matt. 19:24). "You hypocrite, first take the log out of your own eye, and then you will see clearly to take the speck out of your neighbor's eye" (Matt. 7:5). "Do not give what is holy to dogs; and do not throw your pearls before swine, or they will trample them under foot and turn and maul you" (Matt. 7:6). "So whenever you give alms, do not sound a trumpet before you, as the hypocrites do in the synagogues and in the streets, so that they may be praised by others" (Matt. 6:2). "Woe to you, scribes and Pharisees, hypocrites! For you are like whitewashed tombs, which on the outside look beautiful, but inside they are full of the bones of

---

4. Hobbes, *Leviathan*, 38.

5. Bergson, "Laughter," 105.

6. Ryken et al., "Humor," 409.

7. Chesterton, *Orthodoxy*, 153.

the dead and of all kinds of filth" (Matt. 23:27).[8] Such far-fetched imagery is particularly memorable and illuminating.

Early church fathers even turned the incarnation into comic relief, adopting a metaphor of Christ's body as divine bait put on a fishhook (or in a mousetrap) to lure the unsuspecting devil to his demise.[9] Like the white witch in C.S. Lewis's *The Lion, the Witch and the Wardrobe*, who thought she had bound and killed Aslan, the devil is confounded by a deeper magic which soon unravels his seeming victory.[10] "The Devil exulted when Christ died, but by this very death of Christ, the Devil is vanquished, as if he had swallowed the bait in the mousetrap," expounds Augustine. "He rejoiced in Christ's death, like a bailiff of death. What he rejoiced in was then his own undoing."[11] Death couldn't finish off the sinless Christ, for he subsequently triumphed over the forces of darkness by rising from the grave.

Historically, comedy and satire have been categorized into a milder form (following Horace) designed to reform via shame and embarrassment, and a harsher type (following Juvenal) intended to awaken indignation via shock and ridicule.[12] Via comedy we poke fun at self-righteousness and hypocrisy, counteract dogmatism and intolerance, and revel in the playfulness of everyday give-and-take.[13] Among the best agents I know for deflating exalted egos are children. They have such an ingenious way of imitating our signature mannerisms and gestures until we too start to feel that our actions are ludicrous.

As a fallen and fallible Christian, I'm most comfortable with humor directed first at ourselves before it is turned on others, since we all, to a greater or lesser extent, belong to Hypocrites Anonymous. Take that crack by Groucho Marx: "I've had a perfectly wonderful evening, but this wasn't it." As French philosopher Andre Comte-Sponville comments, "Directed toward his hostess after an unsuccessful dinner party, the remark is ironic; delivered to his audience at the close of a performance, it is humorous."[14]

A satirist may disguise himself as a foreigner, reflects literary critic Gilbert Highet, then visit his own country, describing "its customs with

---

8. Trueblood, *Humor of Christ*, 47, 127.

9. Aulen, *Christus Victor*, 47–55.

10. Lewis, *Lion, Witch and Wardrobe*, 145–66.

11. Sanders, *Sudden Glory*, 140.

12. Kiley and Shuttleworth, *Satire*, 23, 28.

13. Hyers, "Comedy," 104–5.

14. Comte-Sponville, *A Small Treatise*, 215.

humorous amazement tempered by disgust,"[15] or paint a picture of another, far-off world to which his own is unfavorably compared.[16] Indeed, a master of satire, Highet decides, "needs a huge vocabulary, a lively flow of humor combined with a strong serious point of view, an imagination so brisk that it will always be several jumps ahead of his readers, and taste good enough to allow him to say shocking things without making the reader turn away in disdain."[17]

Old Testament prophets, usually thought of as stern moralists who rail against Israelite sins, at times can appear more like buffoons. Isaiah goes around Jerusalem barefoot for three years, wearing only a loincloth (like some captive slave), in order to warn of the impending doom of Egypt and Ethiopia, on whom Judah was relying for aid (Isa. 20: 1–6).[18] Ezekiel draws a picture on a clay tablet and constructs toy siege-devices to serve notice of an upcoming military offensive. He lies on his left side behind a model wall for three-hundred and ninety days to represent God's judgment upon Israel and then lies on his right side for forty more days to represent God's judgment upon Judah. He even bakes barley-cakes on cow's dung to symbolize how dire the famine would become. Not only that, he cuts off his hair with a sword, dividing it into thirds to indicate how the inhabitants would suffer: one-third by fire; one-third by the sword; and one-third by a scattering to the wind (Ezek. 4:1—5:4). Such bizarre behavior graphically depicts God's pent-up indignation and the dire consequences.

In 1 Corinthians chapter 1, Paul objects that the sages of this world never came to a genuine knowledge of God, so God revealed himself to humanity by suffering on a cross; such "foolishness" trumps all human presumption. From passages like this, Christians devised a role for the holy fool. "I have offered myself, for some time now, to the Child Jesus, as his *little plaything*," announced nineteenth-century Carmelite nun Therese of Lisieux. "I told him not to use me as a valuable toy children are content to look at but dare not touch, but to use me like a little ball of no value which he could throw on the ground, push with his foot, *pierce*, leave in a corner, or press to his heart if it pleased him."[19] Willing to be pliable, even break the rules of social decorum, we become transparent conduits of his will.

15. Highet, *Anatomy of Satire*, 205.
16. Ibid., 159.
17. Ibid., 242.
18. Scott, *Relevance of the Prophets*, 99.
19. Therese of Lisieux, *Story of a Soul*, 136.

Indeed, humor, satire, and comedy have proven strong weapons in the arsenal of spiritual warfare. After all, what plausible excuse can there be for a life littered by flaws and failure, but that complaint by knight errant Don Quixote: a "malignant enchanter persecutes me, and has put clouds and cataracts into my eyes."[20] To paraphrase Martin Luther, "The best way to drive out the devil, if he will not yield to texts of Scripture, is to jeer and flout him, for he cannot bear scorn."[21] *The Screwtape Letters*, C.S. Lewis's imaginary exchange of letters between an apprentice demon and his seasoned mentor on how to seduce souls, is a supreme example.

In like manner the great Renaissance humorist Rabelais derides that morality more given to homilies than concrete aid. During the fictional cake-peddlers' war, a monk cries out: "Is this any time for talk? You're like the decretalist preachers, who say that whoever sees his neighbor in danger of death ought first, under pain of three-pronged excommunication, to admonish the other to confess and to put himself in a state of grace—all this before giving him any help. And so, after this, when I see them in the river and about to drown, in place of running up to lend them a hand, I intend giving them a good long sermon *de contemptu mundi et fuga saeculi*, on contempt of the world and flight from worldly things, and when they're stiff and dead, that will be time enough to go fish them out."[22]

Is it any wonder then that Richard Milnes, in his memoir of the British satirical poet Thomas Hood, concludes: "[T]he sense of humour is the just balance of all the faculties of man, the best security against the pride of knowledge and the conceits of the imagination, the strongest inducement to submit with a wise and pious patience to the vicissitudes of human existence."[23] Thus, I urge you, my brothers and sisters, laugh your way to heaven.

20. Cervantes, *Don Quixote*, 530.

21. Lewis, *Screwtape Letters*, xv.

22. Rabelais, *Histories of Gargantua and Pantagruel*, 187.

23. Milnes, "Memoir of the Author," xii.

Surprise

When I least expected it,
skyrockets, cloudbursts and dancing lights,
in a word—surprise;
out of the blue
truth knit in a different weave.

All wrapped up in insulation,
decked out in the latest fashion of shock absorbers,
I was unprepared for the perfect crime,
the rape of my innocent complacency.

Startled by a last-minute closing flurry,
my momentum waned,
3-to-1 odds I won't collect today
—a stray bullet felled the Morning Star.

Accidents aren't supposed to happen
in Lucretius, Leibniz and Spinoza,
curved space in a rectangular universe,
a Babylonian jack-in-the-clay.

That's why I live
on a planet that defies prediction,
else all I could do
would be confirm statistics.

Just Suppose—

Just suppose—
the New York Yankees finished last,
the IRS returned your check "Addressee Unknown,"
unicorns nibbled up your tomatoes.

What would happen
if the second law of thermodynamics went on strike,
the baritone was a surgically-induced soprano,
the Kansas plains erupted into firecrackers.

If Jesus turned the wine back into water,
the poison claimed its perpetrator,
bureaucracy could be reduced to its *Urgestalt,*

If freedom could be swapped for Joe Namath,
wildlife preserves housed the pillars of society,
and love blossomed in a eucalyptus tree.

Just suppose your dreams were my reality,
negatives and positives made identical impressions,
and the distance to London varied, depending on the weather.

If the female penetrated deeper than the male,
the cactus thrived in the Arctic tundra,
and a pair of deuces trounced the royal flush,

If mosquitoes could give birth to elephants,
parachutes lowered us softly into stalagmite quarries,
the pigment of our skins could be rinsed and dried overnight.

Priests were ordained via vox populi,
harmonicas replaced symphonies,
and rouge came in twelve different shades of green.

What if thunderstorms could be put on leashes,
Tinker toys fell apart when you're through,
and surgeons could implant soda fizz into radishes,

Doors were put on obelisks,
the square of the hypotenuse of a right triangle
was parallel to the volume of a trapezoid?

Let's pretend
    sows dined at Horn & Hardart,
    God is not greater than his name,
    franking privileges were not available to Anglo-Saxons,
    and buffoons were the earth's unacknowledged legislators.

We might be beyond the looking glass
in the reversible world of Lewis Carroll,
the poetry of the absurd.

I wish I were a soap bubble

I wish I were a soap bubble
wafting out of reach,
cascading an inch or two,
plummeting about a foot.

Oxygen-nitrogen daredevil
pursued by elastic fingertips,
granted life by a plastic tube,
assured of a pinprick doom.

One minute a prism
to bedazzle your adversary,
the next minute invisible
to bewitch the bloodhounds.

Wobbling from circle to ellipse,
prancing and galloping and stopping to breathe,
hanging a curve, drag racing on the straight-away,
exploding on a leaf.

But not before
I became a master contortionist,
curtsied in front of
two applauding elves.

Like the speeding comet
or the glass-bowl goldfish,
what nature revokes in longevity,
she overcompensates with intensity.

Microbes

Tiny, tiny DNA,
miracle of evolution,
cell membrane so resilient,
ultrasonic bursting.

Integrated circuit
no bigger than an angel's wing,
funny face animalcules,
flagella stickum.

Pilus copulation
would horrify your grandmama,
virus promiscuity
would invoke the bishop's censure.

Bathe themselves at 102 degrees Celsius,
incubate at minus 40,
chanson de geste
to the spore and bacterium.

Liquid nitrogen or AC current
rejuvenate ameba,
squish him 100,000 pounds per square inch,
he'll jump right up again.

Adaptable as the bean pod,
stronger than the anvil,
no ganglion or cerebrum,
micrometer protoplasm.

Autotrophic solar panels,
pungent yes! but
they can gobble up
phenol, sawdust, and human waste.

Scavengers, architects,
citric acid and fermentation agents,
Pasteur vs. Winogradsky
—those amazing midgets.

Weeds

It's weeds, I say,
make the whole earth tremble,
pebbles hard as split pea,
chromosome reiteration.

Pull 'em up
and their roots break off.
Hoe 'em
and your field looks overrun by gophers.

Parasite, symbiosis,
dandelion hang gliders,
a plant growing
where I don't want him.

Reproductive madness,
pitchforks and cockleburs
smarter than a PhD,
optimistic about the future.

Ugly? the wild rose
and the morning glory?
Sting they might
after a thousand years of persecution.

I don't mind if
you keep 'em—under glass,
but either get those buggers out of my field
or uncork their potential.

Fall Festival

As flamboyant as the mandrill and the bird-of-paradise,
as muted as the autumn twilight and the aurora borealis,
craving our attention, the maple, the oak,
the birch, and sassafras die so majestically.

What free-floats at its leisure 200 feet or less,
papers the valley with red, yellow and orange humus,
decks the mountain like a baroque Christmas tree,
denudes the xylem and the phloem of their petticoat?

Green deteriorates, polarizing lens brings out the carotenoids,
subliminal hallelujahs, hosannas to the hoarfrost,
veins bulge out to make a shadow print,
stem rudders, a crackling brown powder finale.

As far as the eye can see, the pencil tip of crayolas,
miles of sherbet sundaes, cherry or lemon topping,
backlighting iridescence, side-lighting the mulatto,
alters Dullsville, New Hampshire into month-long carnival.

Nature loves to please cyclically,
accentuates wrinkles every chance she gets,
blossoms to decay, dies for resuscitation,
is as liberal as the nymphomaniac and just as predictable.

the pitter patter of platitudes

The pitter patter of platitudes
disrupts my concentration,
annoys my sensibilities,
wastes my precious time.

The banter about etiquette
somnambulates my being,
provokes a discursive yawn,
delivers an ultimatum of decrepitude.

The hootings of the great horned owl
do seem a bit redundant,
might replace a metronome,
but never buoy my spirits.

By contrast—
the ravings of the orator
alarm my sense of justice,
emotive words can free a felon
and make a laughing-stock of jurors.

The buzzing of the paper wasp
speeds adrenalin to my toes,
creates in me a pacifistic whim
for instant brotherhood.

The honking of the loon-a-tic, nonetheless,
is the most disconcerting,
for instinct cannot yet explain

how Irritation would go into labor
to beget Cooing Harmony.

The Circus

When Barnum & Bailey comes to town,
send Ringling Brothers back to Sarasota Springs:
there'll be cotton-candy babies and five-year-old blimps
running after the pachyderms,
two dwarf clowns imping their way to the big arena,
rubber lips and purple mascara
like third-rate whores from a red-light district.

Three lost fathers ogling half-naked women,
glittering ovals on white-maned palominos,
fire-breathing volcanoes dousing the cheers of children,
devil-may-care gymnasts practicing for a mile-high Olympics,
petite young pencils balancing on a violin gut string,
perpetual motion machines tossing and catching
balls, hockey pucks and ice cream cones,
Herr Barker transmogrifying your hard-earned bucks—
mass psychology to make Dr. Goebbels blush.

Puritans, smash your organs,
Cistercians, go naked like the woodland nymph,
give me that old mass culture
that makes the intelligentsia weep.
So, trainers to your lions!
Snap those whips gaily
till teeth marks ring your severed heads.
Peanuts! Candy-coated ants!
Peanuts! Licorice-flavored doughnuts!

Tigers careening through kerosene hoops,
a chimp with more brains than my aunt Matildi!
haughty seals clapping after their latest performance,
three-ringed extravaganza, calliopes,
painted wagons out of Grimm's fairy tales,
Cannonball Markowitz starting into orbit,
Toothless Oskar, the strongest (-smelling)
man this side of Milwaukee.
Hip, hip, hooray!

Nauseating sideshow freaks, a gorilla
so huge it could crush Pittsburgh before breakfast,
red and green plastic air bubbles,
under the big top it's 90 degrees and smells like a barn.
So laugh all you want,
see if I care,
at least I don't need no psycho-analysis.

The Iowa State Fair

Once a year blue-ribbon Angus,
squealing porkettes and barbecue kings,
Dudelsacks, chameleons, 25-pound gourds,
loquacious clowns wanting a bath.

Self-propelled combines in a minuet,
gyrating pinwheels, honky-tonk arcades,
baby fish kisses, magic lantern shows,
an American flag made out of firecrackers.

Squeeze your girl on the Wild Mouse
and the Ferris wheel, make faces
at each other in a transparent house of glass
—dumbfounded whisper before the three-headed calf.

Horseshoe codgers, honeydew melons, country western hoe-down,
ring the bell, win a cigar,
shoot the owl, take home a stuffed bear,
sign my petition, usher in . . . pandemonium.

Lepidopterous display, feisty brouhaha,
numero uno, egg fu yung,
baby oil, Kiwanis, FFA,
—where's my Shinto waterfall?

Turnip faces, bump-and-go teenyboppers,
I-23, G-54, helicopter rides,
evangelist preaching on the holy Christ rood
—let's go see the swimming competition.

Highway patrol smashes up cars, teaches you how to drive,
a dwarf on stilts, moo-cow going splat,
campaign button: "Do It Again, Ike,"
nostalgia's big down on the farm.

Say five masses for Sister Mary Margaret, the Midwest's first woman clown,
methane extracted from pig manure, alcohol from sugar cane,
Bozo and Greenjeans entertain the tots,
Clark Gable and Bette Davis turn on mom and pop.

Guess your weight? soybean quarter-pounder, blue-green algae ice milk,
45th anniversary of Lawrence and Mrs. Welk,
magnetic ant hills, disappearing water,
Miss America 1952 performs her farewell routine.

Return of King Kong, Betty Boop hit parade—
12-hour cruise on the "Good Ship Lollipop,"
destination memory lane, kitsch kaleidoscope,
escapist Erewhon.

Old Swalm's Store

Old Swalm's store—we bound in like open-mouthed frogs
to this penny arcade of no! no! shout dentists,
Tommy, Sarah and Ken close their eyes and point.

Peppermint macaroons, licorice capsules, bubble gum's waxy jokes,
"Caw! Caw! Sir Henry sailed the Skunk! Mary Stuart's head is chopped!"
the only noise you hear—the clicking rods and cones—a myna bird?

Fill up your stockings with sweetness at the year-round Christmas store,
Pippi Longstocking, Superman, Treasure Isle,
Yipes! there's a hole in my quarter's pocket.

A chartreuse gum drop, an Orioles' baseball card,
grown-up—yes—we—Swalm extends credit till next week's allowance,
"Jawbreakers," "Chocolate kisses," . . . I can do anything mom and dad.

Rub up against the ant farm, a transparent honeycombed hive,
Punch and Judy a penny a ticket,
what this world needs
is a humming good lullaby and an old-fashioned nickel bag of candy.

All Saints' Night

Oh, to be in Dublin on All Saints' Night,
demons step on one another's tails,
fairy wings get clipped in trellises,
Hansel and Gretel cook an old hag stew,
three blind mice shinny up fatso's legs.

Trick or apples, gingerbread men and popcorn balls,
sweet-toothed saints biting off martyrs' heads,
spooks and goblins in flannel or cotton,
door-to-door pygmy Doppler effect.

Might do a spectral analysis to see if they're all carbon-based,
tattered troubadours and courtly ladies,
Laurel & Hardy, Charlie Chaplin mounts Napoleon's stallion,
the witch of Endor, werewolf, Godzilla
and a cluster of enchanted toads—
fists extended like an organ-grinder's chimp.

Neptune and Aphrodite sperming in the foam,
a hobo and a porcupine pulling off a mermaid's fin,
Maid Marian and Friar Tuck pursuing a gargoyle,
the Holy Udder being milked by King Arthur and Sir Gawain.

There's a broomstick sliver of a moon tonight,
priests kneel, Christ harrows the abyss,
cemeteries all abloom, Paradiso removed hence,
the loving tree sighs with bated breath:

The interface of *ecclesia proprius* and *ecclesia universalis*,
spirit and matter interchange,
acres and acres of intergalactic matter,
one night all hell converges.

To Collar a Leprechaun

Pour salt on his tail,
catch his reflection,
camouflage his shadow,
pepper his lair with lucky charms,
recite the "Pater Noster"
standing on your head.

Rattle the chivaree bells,
mix radioactive iodine with his beer,
pour luminescent paint about his bath-hole,
set out chocolate-covered castor oil,
mimic his mating yelp, find him a pixie,
write the Tetragrammaton in the shape of a magic square.

Let him snooze on Vulcan's cushion,
steam up his favorite mushroom,
squirt out Elmer's epoxy,
say "abracadabra" over his hangnail,
immolate a voodoo,
place your finger on his Ouija,
prepare the newt and toe of frog.

There's a shaded no man's land bordering science and religion,
an incubator for quacks and pseudo-cults,
here no law seems to hold,
every thought is a leap of faith.

Pluto's Realm

When into Pluto's realm I go,
I need my rubbers and my stole,
grottoes, dripstones and organ pipes,
travertine, pools, and aragonite.

Slippery rocks, and blind fish do swim,
optimists throw pennies and slim
folk squeeze their stomachs in,
bats scowl and lost rivers recognize their sin.

Mammoth, Carlsbad, Rieseneishöhle,
ice age den, first art shöwle,
keep time by the water clock,
observe the seasons at the mossy rock.

Where's my periscope? No Cambridge white
or Walden blue when it's 55 degrees perennially,
stalactites and stalagmites mate
only after their 2,534th date.

Orchestral Romance

The violin is infatuated
with the cello,
the French horn
is eyeing the bashful tuba,
and the trombone is sliding
toward the marimba.

Love's Investor

A penny for a kiss,
A shilling for a squeeze,
A quarter for a twining rendezvous,
A dollar toward the head.

Love can be audited,
Payables and receivables
have their fleshly counterparts,
What eagerness to fall into the red!

Tabulate the most vital figures,
Project reasonable dividends,
Comb the inventory with microscopic eyes,
Demand a five-year statement.

First column: "Celibate or Partner,"
The second: "Loan or Investment,"
Third: "Adjustments for Growth,"
The bottom line? A pregnant egg.

Consult your accountant before final signature,
Sink it all in one dubious bout,
Offer your heart as collateral,
Analyze liquidity, write off liabilities,
—and forget about romantic notions of merger!

What Can I Offer?

What can I offer a noble prince:
    shall I sacrifice my heart?
And how will I seal my passion's vow,
    but with an icon kiss?
When do we sleep two to a bed
    —after the Father's blessing?
And where may I find a second gallant
    now that I've vanquished one?

Baby's Playpen

Origami tigers, soft, molded elephants,
mechanical barking dogs,
tweed cobras that can be picked up and squeezed,
plastic nipples which suck air.
No wonder his whole body yawns.

Baby—Me?

I peer into a dusty mirror
and shrink back almost to a midget
    —is that me in the fluid embryo?
       did I invariably cry
           when my mother removed her nipple?
    gurgle below my shining mobile?
       burden others with the disposal of smelly diapers?
go around chewing on couch, chair, wallpaper,
              stomp on poor puppy's tail?

Was I such a peevish rascal
    as to keep others awake
              if I wasn't fed proper?
          giving out an enigmatic Mona Lisa smirk
   before teasing relatives?
          blabbering to myself
      in a cataleptic, psychosomatic trance?
                  Unaware pain is surely within,
seeing no difference between strangers,
    juju masks and my own papa,
         is this helpless, unsophisticated blob—me?

                 I wonder—
            where are his philosophy books?
            his gorgeous blond curls and bone-perfect teeth?
       Don't tell me he's asexual
    and doesn't even notice his aunt's puckering lips?

I know he wants to build a Palladian villa,
but his foam blocks won't stay put,
he can't even keep his head from wobbling.

Come on now, baby,
compose that Mozart sonata,
spout conic sections like Pascal,
why spend the whole day long
trying to turn over—
what difference can it possibly make
whether you goo-goo on your stomach
or flip-flop on your back?

All you want
is peek-a-boo and lullabies,
you hold your picture book upside down
like a piece of minimalist art.
Hey! Wait a minute!
Now there's something.
You do everything nutty,
learn your lessons two months late.
oh brother!
You've a wonderful life ahead.

But for now the world would be pleased
if you took a longish nap.
It's not quite ready
to be jarred, scrunched, tweaked,
shoved under your looking-glass (catty-cornered).
It can wait to be dissected
a wee-ee bit longer.

In the Womb

If I could go back to the womb again
where the sweetest juices flowed,
I had my own epidermal covering
and a placenta around my head.

Undeveloped I bound about my jelly sphere,
like a leech I sup upon my host,
half-fish, half-mammal—vertebrates display such teeth—
all boundaries are persuasive, foes diminutive.

In the fetal crouch injury is abated,
you're not conspicuous nor singled out,
maternal pity falls like Yosemite mists,
you can't get lost, all oxygen is purified.

No boss to brandish pink slips,
no sibling rivals,
you're suspended in a buoyant solution,
don't have to "prove" yourself, you're obvious to all.

In der Weltkuh ist die Milch frei,
the decor moist and dark,
independence is an illusion,
past sins all but washed away.

You let out a kick for sheer joy,
no one scolds,
and if you're sick of being pampered,
exit early, no one screams.

You twitch about in a dream bubble,
love is squishably soft,
all instincts are still secure
and you've eons to reform.

Backfloatin'

Insomniac
in a hammock
made of waves,
biorhythms relaxing
in the eye of a hurricane,
water lapping
up to your temple,
a cumulus tissue
to shield
your cornea,
vision blurred
like a Dali-scape,
ears attuned
to soluble shrieks—
rest easily on
your arched back.

Sensations all askew
when half a lake
swims up your nose.
Cough it up—
and still be a gentleman?
But your throat's
as deep as the regal lily,
your eyes well up
like the morning after—
sweet serenity
duped so violently.

But next Sunday
more of the same,
backfloat till
your stomach's red,
eyes shut to
parabolic declension,
until savagely interrupted
by "the park's about to close."
Pinpoint your exact
center of gravity,
vibrate to nature's pulse,
ascertain the various
shades of blue,
take note of the blending
of sky and tree,
pry into the closing
of your pores—
or just about any excuse
so you don't have
to clean your room.

Summer Heat

Dizziness alternating with heat exhaustion,
sea breezes propping up my lack of resolve,
the new Elvis begins a new craze,
rattlers slither under a cactus stalagmite—
estivating their life away,
if only I had gills like Aquaman
I'd amuse myself at some Coney Island Atlantis,
X-rays, gamma rays, ultraviolet burns,
maybe I'd rather vacation on Pluto.

Bikini-clad bronze statues laid
to rest under bumbershoots,
swabbed in acrid Indian sunblock,
more free flesh than an X-rated booth.
Tell Re to wheel back his chariot,
sweat oozes down my frontal lobe,
some cool liquid giving me stomach cramps.

Air conditioners disrupting an entire block's siesta,
the pavement simmers beneath my canvas shoes,
impetuous drivers are determined that
one more blast from their horn
will unsnarl a 12-block traffic jam,
the elderly swoon in unlicensed nursing homes,
children do a rain dance before their local fire hydrant,
lemonade man on the corner leaks
ice water into the nearest gutter.

Puppy love hatches on a Ferris wheel,
pubic hairs ruffled in the back seat of a Toyota,
dad missing church with a triple-bogey on No. 8,
two 16-foot campers sputtering up Pike's Peak,
a black-and-brown dachshund panting to and fro
for no particular reason.
Two pranksters yelling "Shark! Shark!"
clearing out the water for a quarter of a mile,
and lazy me climbing into the tub
for my third shower since breakfast.

A Modern Mother Goose

Little Tommy Dirigible
played his trombone so bellicose
that Herr Pate's toupee was requisitioned
from an orchestra seat to the balcony
of grandfather's handlebar mustache;
at the same time it generated cyclonic activity
among the petticoats in the second floor ladies' lounge,
barometric pressure dips a full hundred meters from the epicenter—
an eye which could whoosh in Jericho's facade.

The Onrushing Yellow Tide

The onrushing yellow tide
crouches between pompom, bespangled miniskirts
at a mass pep rally
where the dominant cheer is beer,
first the ongoing projectile hesitates,
then through the middle, around the end, tossed in the air,
four plays later the dirigible is punted and downed,
whistles blow, helmeted gladiators huddle,
butting rams lock horns,
while one fleet back sneaks across the Maginot Line
carrying the sacred blimp
which opponents seek to flatten.

All afternoon victory swings between these two galloping sets of spikes,
coaches map out T- and Y-formations,
scouts look for chinks, wounds in the defense,
crowds roar first approval, then disgust,
time is called,
popcorn and soda pop spatter down your sweater,
tee-ra, shaboom, shabang,
clenched fists shout: "Tar and feather the quarterback! Fire the coach!"
the score goes up by sacred sevens,
when the guns go off Achaean heroes are borne aloft on litters,
Troy goats hung up in effigy like punctured puppets.

So this is what Thomas Arnold imagined built up a boy's character?
what demagogue could have invented a stranger show of shows!

The Dodo

The stupid-looking dodo
is deficient in his brain and horned bill,
the ignoramus stands with one foot up,
his expression straight out of a cartoon book,
the numbskull pecks a stupid peck,
flies a god-awful short trajectory,
a phrenologist would locate
the malady on the left side
of his feathered head,
among relatives he feels inferior,
his ancestors have intermarried
to the point of imbecility,
with peers he's depressed,
unassertive, embarrassed to speak,
there are rumors his habits
have been catalogued, revised,
debated, followed-up,
but chiefly the findings
derive from his name,
a shallow, unfortunate misnomer
he'll never live down,
yes, he is extinct.

Life Is in the Blood

Life is in the blood, you know,
if you don't believe me:
saw off your head
and watch it flow.
(Repeat dosage twice daily).

Indifference

The bastion of indifference
situated on ho-hum promontory
is almost impregnable by normal means.

Bait

Bright plumage on a hook
luring drab fish
to bite metal.

Whodunit?

The waitress looks suspicious
with her darting eyes and tight, twisting derriere,
but then the lieutenant had the weapons training
and the motive of old boy revenge,
yet the professor was a livid sot
and after each Bloody Mary
shouted, "Smith be hanged!"

Then the victim's mistress was a jealous sort
and didn't appreciate the actress butting in,
though the Mafioso was not known for his inhibitions,
the former police detective could have done it
just to keep in cardiovascular shape,
perhaps the dentist's wife had the most to lose
if the blackmailer revealed her sister's whereabouts.

The business executive might have been protecting
his illegal offshore monopoly,
the precinct captain frequently accepted bribes at Sixth and Main
and could have been tipped off by his underworld informer,
the male stripper wasn't getting any younger
and might have felt his chances for love were fading fast,
the boxer had been in trouble with the law before
and was afterwards seen visiting his boyhood chum, the priest,
the cabby, too, was up to his eyeballs in allegations.

The doorman has been known to push a few tenants about,
even the cripple across the street could become rowdy
if his wife didn't arrive home on time,

what of the mayor? he could be involved in a payoff or cover-up,
why exempt the president?
was he trying to prevent some international incident?

Or maybe Smith was just the whipping boy for some rival gang,
a decoy to set investigators off the trail;
it's true that two shady figures were last seen in a '68 Barracuda
heading south on Broadway,
having narrowly missed a female pedestrian;
but why were there no fingerprints on the steering wheel, the chrome,
    the dash?
what was the angle and size of the wound, according to the pathologist,
could it have been self-inflicted?

Have your alibis ready—
for in the world of Raymond Chandler
everyone is a suspect,
or at least looks sufficiently guilty
until his innocence is proven contrariwise;
to entertain the jaded public
the plot should twist like the lower Mississippi.

You, reader, don't be surprised
if you're under suspicion, about to be interrogated,
don't you have a few skeletons peeping out the closet?
in the end the author may clamp the cuffs on your wrists,
since, after all, aren't you the victim Abel's brother?
hiding behind that Mr. Clean look,
Philip Marlowe wasn't fooled,
the judge may let you out early for good behavior.

Are There Universes?

Are there universes beyond or beside our own,
    bounded more by imagination than planetary gravity,
where truth varies with the coefficient of light,
    bonsai plants wreak havoc with the dwarf ecology,
nebulous Plato can be scooped up off the grass,
    time runs in circles around its five-dimensional counterparts.

Electromagnetic force-fields disintegrate at 10 to the minus 7th power,
    where mechanistic hands whir on self-regenerating fuels,
androids ravage or inseminate one another's wombs,
    nudity's in fashion and pinstripes go to the electric chair,
four walls a room completes, no ceilings or a floor,
    like a chuckwalla which blows up to infinity.

Carolling is a form of exercise that only angels doubt,
    man is perfect, just his environment has failed,
cleanliness is greater than godliness since obedience is the norm,
    everything is animate, even the toys trot off to work,
east o' the sun, west o' the moon, carrots blush,
    planets revolve in triangles around polygon stars.

Water is brighter the deeper you snorkel
    and the oxygen/carbon-dioxide cycle is lethal to all,
there are no stratagems of war,
    orchids suck nutrients off the asteroids,
intelligent life amuses itself on cosmic bergs,
    while starships float past a menagerie of incomparable plenitude.

The World of a Raindrop

In the world of a raindrop
is more life than I dare count,
on the choir loft of a pinhead
a thousand angels squawk,
after the explosion of a proton
the entire history of ideas will evolve.

First a kernel, then a blade,
at last a stalk and full-ripe ear,
an insolent gray follicle
causes many a maiden to snuffle,
after one overwrought phrase
flotillas and armored divisions go forth.

The smallest candle can allure
the luna moth's vacant eyes,
Troy capitulated hard upon
Paris' lust for Helen's heart,
to Adam . . . the fruit of good and evil
was a trifling thing.

Grammar

Synonyms juggling for position,
prefixes double-parked,
twords copulating without my permission,
a gerund stuck out like a f
                              i
                                s
                                   h
                                      i
                                         n
                                           g

                                              r
                                               o
                                               d.

Nouns repeating out of boredom
or for the sake of symmetry,
active verbs jumping off the   page,
passive ones a steamroller couldn't budge;
cuneiform or hieroglyphs
more fun than the Phoenician alphabet.

Pronouns substituting for their predecessors,
infinitives split and then make up,
prepositions who'll latch onto any old noun,
adverbs playing musical chairs with adjectives,
proper nouns demanding Capitalization,
abstract concepts possessing syntactic bodies,
commas taking a breather.

Exclamation points flagging down rapid eye movement,
question marks giving you a chance to reply,
apostrophes filling in for letters on vacation,
periods and paragraphs, Ptolemaic grid,
subject-verb-object, object-verb-subject,
shuttle diplomacy, irreversible solution:
scientific precision, a grammarian's absurdity.

Hyphen, dash's little brother,
white space so the whole page
isn't crossword squiggles,
imperative and indicative:
flighty verbs always changing moods,
subjunctive and optative, degrees of possibility
—all have problems with the fourth dimension.

Male and female nomenclature?
singular or plural integers?
letters double-up when they want a little action,
nouns declining, verbs conjugating,
adding tails or cutting off their noses,
stems and roots and loose connections,
inflections and accents too subjective to bother with
—it's a haphazard maze, Herculean gauntlet,
a structuralist's nightmare.

I Envy You, Montaigne

I envy you, Montaigne,
your head crammed full of
Greek and Latin quotations,
your Bordeaux constituency,
I envy you, your leisure,
your uncommon, common reason,
that ability to extrapolate
from the meanest shard
of primate self-consciousness,
your lexicographer-honeyed tongue,
a tolerance and a sensitivity
beyond that enlightened age,
your encyclopedic fancy,
that rigorous, unbiased look within,
an optimistic/pessimistic balance,
a love for undulating people
but distaste for their masks,
I envy you your Epictetus cool
pleasing restraint, wizardous literary polish,
your autobiographically sincere
dedication to art which instructs,
instinct for what's real
and will last, and naturally enough,

I envy your place on my shelf,
one I wish had been labeled:
"Bazyn, essayist, American."

The Charlatan

I abhor,
most of all,
the charlatan.

Wants me and you's money
for some pernicious reason,
slithers away from the glaring bulb
to some less conspicuous cranny.

If you're for evil, stand up for it!
Don't give me no placebo
or paint yourself up like Good King Wenceslas.
Be proud of your wretched occupation.

Ask God to bless
your five moldy loaves and two rotten fish
and to multiply the stinking bread cast upon the waters.
Uneasy consciences are for fools.

Fence-sitters should be
taken out and shot,
divided juries hung,
irresolution rectified.

And what of you,
the indecisive businessman,
by day pure as the effervescent brook,
at night murky as the flooded Missouri?

Aspire now toward your robber baron ideal!
Not enthusiastic for sons and followers?
Think illegal means are unworthy of their ends?
Disinterested goods are an abomination!

Facades merely encourage schizophrenia,
the cloak of respectability
means alms for middlemen.
Or are you in it for the schemes

and treachery? Not to march
lemmings to the nearest cove,
but to watch the lambs bleat helplessly?
Roundabout depravity.

Too calculated, too delayed
for my gratification, I'll have
my evil and I'll have it now (thank you).
Otherwise, God might teach me patience.

Caveat Emptor

Frauds, hucksters, quacks
trying to make a dollar out of 95 cents:

"This model doesn't come with a guarantee,
but that one for $30 more will last a lifetime.

"Sorry, sir, the sale ended yesterday.
Besides, we're temporarily out of stock,
try us again next year.

"I know the merchandise was advertised for $1.98,
but postage and handling costs $7.83.

"The gift wrapping will be $3 more,
4% city tax, $6 for the limited warranty,
$2.50 for the carrying case, $8 for an extra set of refills . . . .

"Defective copy? Impossible!
We have twelve quality checks.

"No exchange without a sales slip!
No complaints without a notarized affidavit!

"Deceptive advertising? What's the matter—
you can't read the fine print?

"We'll match or beat any price in town
—except that store's. They violate state labor practices.

"I'm afraid we already cashed your check.
What! You mailed it this morning?

"That scale does, too, work,
I just weighed my grandson on it.

"Did you sit on the box all the way home?
The item is fire-resistant, but you can't use a blowtorch.

"Yeah, we pride ourselves on friendly service.
What of it?"

If all else fails:
caveat emptor.

Delicate Things

I'm in love with delicate things,
        a finch's serenade,
        a black mesh stocking,
        an envelope fresh sealed,
        an atomizing Alsace cologne.

I'm in love with miniature
        busts and replicas,
        proportionate scale globes,
        midget dogs and parakeets,
        a leprechaun and gnome.

I'm in love with what's imaginary,
        enchanted roads to Ithaca,
        fictional memoirs and diaries,
        a crazy, slanting twist,
        not some blunt stock repertoire.

I'm in love with exotic
        Oriental climes,
        cultures which diverge sharply from our own,
        the primitive/ancient/medieval,
        mystic strands of metaphor.

I'm also in love with the eternal,
        Aristotle's *primum mobile*,
        a unified field theory of matter,
        all things which converge and form a whole,
        and especially, you, God, the singular absolute.

God's Mercy

There's a two-pronged bridge sticking out into infinity,
spanning the noumenal and sensory spheres,
freeways weave in and then disappear,
cars disintegrate in the twilight zone of love.

Opaque curtain shrouds welded links,
which Faith acknowledges and Reason scorns,
angels descending Jacob's slippery ladder,
touching terra firma and scurrying up again.

Must virtue require a battlefield
where each genre of skill can be assessed—
close-ups, wide-angles and 500 mm. telephotos?
Or does God take on meaner forms *persona incognito*?

Avatars mediating between sense and nonsense,
Gnostic emanations streaming from Plato's hole,
mirages reflecting each other in perfect precision,
the Bread and Wine crucified for our indifference.

Let God's mercy have its fling,
organ-grinder of righteousness,
excellence resides not in mere aristocrats,
but hath a democratic tinge.

Thank you, God

Thank you, God,
for dappled gray
and scarlet polka-dots,
for natural curls
and coagulants,
for the still unborn fetus
and graveside chrysanthemums,
for the terra firma
and the Crab Nebula.

Thank you for every grace
this planet knows:
for bobolinks
and rainbow hues,
for the ozone layer
and electro-magnetic force fields,
for krill, crayolas and kryptonite.

For every bloated body
you've rescued from starvation,
for arthritic hands
still capable of work,
for pointed breasts
and open-and-shut thighs,
for lollipops, fudgesicles
and IBM computers.

For Edison, Gutenberg,
and the Neolithic Revolution,

for natural selection
and beneficent mutations,
for early frosts
and pestilences—not
directly caused by you,
El-Elohe-Israel—
I'll wager that French mathematician you're real.

For microscopic fragments
of revelation,
for creating, upholding, sustaining
this infinitesimal universe—
through pleading and persuasion
it might redound to its original purpose,
complete the redemption
only just begun
—and defrock those presumptuous few
who stand in the way.

If the Kingdom Comes

If the Kingdom comes, let it not be with gongs or sonic booms,
    tiaras, vestments, or endowments from state,
let it not arrive in crystal naves or via soapbox pulpits,
    screened Eucharists or "I Love Jesus" posters.

If the Kingdom shows, may it not be with charismatic hoopla,
    perfumed relics or in a stained glass entourage,
let it not materialize in mercenary choirs or meditative prayer,
    in St. Antony cells or due to self-flagellation.

If the Kingdom is manifest, please, not in Lourdes or Constantinople,
    at parish council or during ecumenical crusades,
let it not emerge during bingo, women's society, or fall fair,
    in Vulgate exegesis, patristic allusions, or lectern anecdotes.

If the Kingdom appears, let it be an acrobatic revue,
    or fester in cynic Diogenes' tub,
let it crack mirrored hearts, appall parochial justice,
    have it dangle from baby's hands or her toes.

Since Earth Has Cooled

Since earth has cooled,
her vigor's depleted,
molten beauty sags,
time itself stands and waits.

Then does Jehovah
fling his sperm
into the virgin's lap
to bear earth's groans.

All toothless and sad,
a Sphinx wrapped in an enigma,
the Almighty dependent
on fragile, doubting hands.

The child sucks and wets,
attempts human games,
is scolded and punished,
made the anti-Semitic butt.

Grown to manhood
he wields an enchanter's flame,
earth is reinvigorated,
weary old man given an elastic heart.

A Desert Father

Steeped in holiness
from foot to crown,
I climb plateau after plateau
to a still uninhabited rung,
men call me *Abba, Starets*,
lick my dripping dung,
yes, so I am,
except for this bevy of dancing girls.

The Reliquary

That grandest of all relics—
the head of John the Baptist
preserved in champagned vinegar.

Jesting Angels

Jesting angels, baroque cherubs, flaming sirens,
bodies unincorporated, eyes glued on God,
errand-boys, wills merged with the sublime,
pokers in the ashes of man's Yuletide stubble,
wear Perseus helmets in our atmosphere,
the sole witnesses to Houdini's sepulcher escape,
tourists or ambassadors from a kingdom of all 7's,
spheroids with three-dimensional translucency.

Winged mites two-stepping on a pinprick or celestial puff balls,
harpsichord heralds bellowing the high mass,
carry the cornucopia of blessings, upset-fruit-basket their favorite sport,
(when you hear the thunder, 'tis but the angels' disco madness
and the lightning their psychedelic flares,
rainbows, their luminescent-stroked tattoos)
funky angels dam up Nature's law as whimsy, temporarily
    suspending physics,
inveterate buffoons, play hide-and-seek among the asteroids,
slay dragons with their plastic swords,
feast on inanimate matter and drink only mineral water,
invented Esperanto,
are anxious to peer into salvation, which they know not existentially.

Lucifer cordoned off Hades, commandeered a train of prison mates,
in one fell swoop redirected a motley angel band
to the hottest spot in three quadrants,
at cross purposes to God's directive will
they seduce mortal women to hatch a brood of giants,
parrot the Morning Star in sheer derision

like God's own damnèd ape,
crack sinners: fireball moving targets,
scorch innocent humanoids.
What great temptation could Lucifer invoke
to bid their felicity expire short term?
Bite the bullet.

The Geneva Watchmaker

God, the Geneva watchmaker,
Jesus, the Nuremberg Egg.

Art Thou the One?

Art thou the one the temple rent,
healed the nymphomaniac,
called twelve pupils to hail the evangel?
Was herded before the procurator,
stretched out on an I-beam,
pitied and encased in Joseph's sepulcher?

The same that confounded the rabbis,
was anointed by the headless prophet,
compelled his disciples be cannibals?
Maligned for insurrection,
lacerated as a scapegoat,
cheated by his treasurer?

Art thou the victor or the victim
in your manly pilgrimage—
sublimitas or humility?
Radical kenosis,
a tripping stone to the Gnostic,
a logical impossibility for Aristotle.

Nature + Grace = Hypostatic Union,
triad, three personae, tritheism?
Two wills, two equivalent natures,
one telescopic purpose?
Phantom, freak,
or stuffed with God-consciousness?

Exemplar, companion,
or deluded visionary?
Reformer, recluse,
or miracle-working celebrity?
Poet, preacher,
or enigmatist?

God knows
the contradictions
you've somehow fused together.
May we pattern ourselves
into your holographic likeness.

The Recumbent Christ

Christ napped in the hull,
while his disciples ran helter-skelter
securing nets, reinforcing sails,
clamping down whatever was not flying loose,
Christ turned over in a dreamy sort of smile
when Peter put on his wetsuit,
hurling a fist toward the piled-high nimbus,
agitated that his life's investment would soon be lost.

Christ managed a decided yawn
when Andrew shook his recumbent form,
motioning like a dumb demoniac that his dinghy would soon be swamped,
forlornly scanning the horizon for that reassuring arc,
Christ rubbed the cobwebs from his bleary eyes long enough
to watch the church launch ratcheting inquisitions, swaggering crusades,
then petition for reinforcements: legions of destroying angels,
who like some revolutionary Kohlhaas would take up hatchets, pitchforks,
    and knives.

At last he became cognizant of the hubbub on his left periphery,
opened up his magical, mystery hands,
faith just didn't seem to comfort these anxious, seething types,
perhaps he could somehow relate exempla drawn from lilies or sparrows,
but right now all he wanted was a few more z's.

Walter Mitty Sin

I vowed never to forsake Jesus,
to acknowledge him
even if accusers drag me
before kings and executioners,
though my body be stretched on a quivering rack
and I be tormented by the tyrant's red-hot forks,
toadies fasten electrodes to my earlobes,
remove my prattling tongue, gouge out my pleading eyes,
I be dunked into boiling, brackish oils,
buried feet up in the burning Gobi sands,
fed chunk-by-chunk to hungry lions, placed up to my armpits
    with stinging ants,
had my virility put to the test—unweaponed—across from
    seasoned gladiators,
been tied to a stake, lit up like a Hanukkah candelabrum,
placed in a shivering barracks on the tundra with no kindling or soulmate
—yet I will not deny my precious Savior.

Though envious bystanders label me feeble-minded, sodomite,
I be called Ishmael, pariah, prison camp stoolie,
rival parties besmirch me as a Procopius turncoat or fomenter of riots,
preachers publicly denounce my feigning adherence to the fundamentals,
evangelists wonder whether I'm one of the chosen or one of the damned,
neighbors consider my Sabbath attendance a pious bluff,
agnostics see me as one given to self-delusions
which pull me away from vital social and economic concerns,
co-religionists declare what counts is God—not his name,
still will I hold allegiance to you, Yeshua bar-Joseph.

Though I fall in full-view of my immediate family,
and the Devil delight in tormenting my conscience with secret sin
    after secret sin,
I start to doubt any inkling of coherence or symmetry,
consider the righteous emaciated fanatics,
while coddled sinners feast with their mistresses in ivory mansions,
though the world be given over to evil for a thousand generations,
blaspheming panderers parade as bishops in fleecy vestments
which would deceive the very elect,
henceforth I will cling to the innocent blood of Abel—
at least until the cock crows thrice and I weep bitter Petrine tears—
for that Walter Mitty sin of imagined boldness.

Hustling Toward Jerusalem

Unstoppered love,
grace on top of grace,
righteousness held in check by mercy,
champagne people, bubbling over
lutes for the holy dove,
drape the chapel in purple and green,
light candles for his second coming,
let the child out to frolic,
coax a little adolescent humor,
laugh like pilgrims hustling toward Jerusalem,
get drunk on God.

Beautiful are the hands
suspending mosaics in the temple air,
flinging open the gates of adoration,
bounding up to the communion rail,
miter the lily with a Magdalene flask,
stuff a shamrock up the cockleshell,
place Barbara's tower in Bernard's beehive,
pitch Lucy's eyes at the winged ox,
let hedonism be, good-bye, good-bye to Increase Mather.

Then give an account
of every joy repudiated
before the Savior clown.
Besmirch the cotton candy with a Celtic cross,
Epiphany has turned to Lent.

A Sunday School Lesson

I didn't see Christ laugh
when a demoniac oinked among the swine—
while fuming at prods and sticks,
suffered bruises and cuts above his harelip.

I never even saw Jesus chuckle
when legions of decency lifted high a harlot's skirt,
buffoons rushed in, unsheathed paper penises,
self-righteous townspeople kept spitting out lewd accusations.

Christ didn't seem to get the joke
when children catcalled "Crybaby," "Nincompoop," "Cripple,"
refused to let strangers join in their fatuous games,
welcomed like a clam those of a different limp.

Christ never turned to smile
when a bashful girl stuttered, lisped, mispronounced her name,
a ragged orphan begged for scraps of bread,
a distraught mother whimpered over her delinquent child.

I never saw him pantomime, jibe, or mimic,
wear the ass's cap and bells,
not aspiring to be the world's greatest comedian,
Christ never made fun at someone else's expense.

A New Orleans Funeral

I want a New Orleans funeral,
brass bands, ragtime,
tall tales to amuse the corpse,
cry at the birth, laugh at the death,
the snare drum grants relief
from last month's rent.

When I lay ma' body down
and Jesus whispers to ma' soul,
Lor', will you pick up them mangled pieces
and grant all a Mardi Gras?

I wanna shout Salvation
from a pine box vault,
go ridin' in mas'sa Ezekiel's chariot,
angels composin' spirituals,
clappin', stompin' like Zaire cantors
crisscrossin' the glossolalia aisles.

My burden is mighta' heavy,
my sins a bushel and a peck,
only grace and overcomer's mercy
can wipe away the hurt.

I wanna join that eternal circle,
exchange a few remarks with brother Saul,
feast on cosmic attributes,
check ma' name against a gold-

leaf book, when the roll is called,
bojangle with David before the ark.

Won't have to kiss Satan's posterior no mo,'
won't have to do battle with the rascally progeny of Eve,
I'll be reconstituted
seamless as a jazz trombone.

A Beatnik View of the Ascension

Christ climbed up another way,
while his disciples were gazing
at the overcast skies above bourgeois Galilee,
Christ escaped via a circuitous route,
the crowds who had known his healing touch
put on their Sunday suits and stylish Easter bonnets,
wore their most pious, silly smiles,
then focused their telescopic pupils upwards
to scan for roving angel bands,
musicians pressed near in hopes of overhearing
harmonies beyond the eight-tone scale,
others were eager to caress his splendiferous, mystic light
or view a flashing extraterrestrial vehicle
emitting some universal *bios* code.

Naturally one and all thought a juggler or acrobat
would entertain before Christ's dress rehearsal,
assumed God would fill up a helium balloon
with gold doubloons to sprinkle among the faithful,
that Jesus would utter some saccharine homily concerning peace and goodwill,
adherence to family values, respect for governing authorities,
but tired of their miracle-grubbing fingers
he took the backstairs to the upper chamber,
a rickety old man came out to say, "How do,"
a pristine white dove perched on his shoulder,
then the three wrung their collective foreheads, frowned,
decided to wait for another, more pliable species.
Christ would have liked to come again,
but the froth and the adulation were enough to kill a lesser man.

The Peaceable Kingdom

In the peaceable kingdom on death's other shore
    Aslan reigns in Narnia,
all who walk through the gates are one.

Like a polyphonic scale trout sing,
    two warriors glance, then tip their swords,
the Hammurabic code reads, "Caritas."

The frustrations I miss, also the entanglements,
    the alka-seltzer intervals,
the sickness and the horrors that made my conscience bleed.

Oh, to be in that Imperial City as placid as an April swan,
    chastely flutter my wings,
mount up in a gingham vertigo.

Grievances and mistrust—Gone!—rivers of lamentation dried up,
    the soul basks and waltzes in anticipation,
God coquettishly unveils the plumage of paradise.

The tiger and the fawn dream in one another's arms,
    yin and yang are agreeably measured out,
joy cross-reflected, multiplied a trillion-fold.

Like Pliny's chameleon all neither eat nor drink but walk on air,
    here, says Isaiah, the mirage becomes a pool,
the body rises spherical in a festival of lights.

Angels conduct seminars, you sow and reap in a single hour,
     spiritual bodies jet forth between the molecules,
and a little child experiences the beatific vision.

Recommended Resources on Humor and Christianity

Brandt, Sebastian. *The Ship of Fools*. Translated by Edwin H. Zeydel. New York: Dover, 1962.

Bakhtin, Mikhail. *Rabelais and His World*. Translated by Helene Iswolsky. Bloomington: Indiana University Press, 1984.

Berger, Peter L. *Redeeming Laughter: The Comic Dimension of Human Experience*. New York: Walter de Gruyter, 1997.

Carroll, Lewis. *Alice's Adventures in Wonderland & Through the Looking-Glass*. New York: New American Library, 1962.

Cervantes, Miguel de. *The Adventures of Don Quixote*. Translated by J.M. Cohen. Baltimore: Penguin, 1970.

Chaucer, Geoffrey. *The Canterbury Tales*. Translated by Ronald L. Ecker and Eugene J. Crook. Palatka: Hodge & Braddock, 1993.

Chesterton, G.K. *Orthodoxy*. San Francisco: Ignatius, 1995.

Erasmus, Desiderius. *Praise of Folly and Letter to Marten Van Dorp, 1515*. Translated by Betty Radice. New York: Penguin, 1993.

Highet, Gilbert. *The Anatomy of Satire*. Princeton: Princeton University Press, 1972.

Huizinga, Johan. *Homo Ludens: A Study of the Play-Element in Culture*. Boston: Beacon, 1951.

Kierkegaard, Soren. *Parables of Kierkegaard*. Edited by Thomas C. Oden. Princeton: Princeton University Press, 1989.

Lewis, C.S. *The Screwtape Letters*. New York: Bantam, 1982.

Niebuhr, Reinhold. "Humor and Faith." In *The Essential Reinhold Niebuhr*, edited by Robert McAfee Brown, 49–60. New Haven: Yale University Press, 1986.

Rabelais, Francois. *The Histories of Gargantua and Pantagruel*. Translated by J.M. Cohen. New York: Penguin, 1978.

Swift, Jonathan. *The Portable Swift*. Edited by Carl Van Doren. New York: Viking, 1963.

Sanders, Barry. *Sudden Glory: Laughter as Subversive History*. Boston: Beacon, 1995.

Trueblood, Elton. *The Humor of Christ*. New York: Harper & Row, 1975.

Works Cited

Aristotle. "Parts of Animals." Translated by W. Ogle. In *The Complete Works of Aristotle: The Revised Oxford Translation, Volume 1*, edited by Jonathan Barnes, 1049. Princeton: Princeton University Press, 1991.

Aulen, Gustaf. *Christus Victor*. Translated by A.G. Hebert. New York: Macmillan, 1986.

Bergson, Henri. "Laughter." Translated by Cloudesley Brereton and Fred Rothwell. In *Comedy*, introduced by Wylie Sypher, 105. New York: Anchor, 1956.

Cervantes, Miguel de. *The Adventures of Don Quixote*. Translated by J.M. Cohen. Baltimore: Penguin, 1970.

Chesterton, G.K. *Orthodoxy*. San Francisco: Ignatius, 1995.

Comte-Sponville, Andre. *A Small Treatise on the Great Virtues*. Translated by Catherine Temerson. New York: Metropolitan Books, 2001.

Cooper, Howard. "Humour." In *The Alphabet of Paradise*, 63. Woodstock, Vermont: Skylight Paths, 2003.

Highet, Gilbert. *The Anatomy of Satire*. Princeton: Princeton University Press, 1972.

Hobbes, Thomas. *Leviathan*, edited by J.C.A. Gaskin. Oxford: Oxford University Press, 1996.

Hyers, Conrad, "Comedy." In *New and Enlarged Handbook of Christian Theology*, edited by Donald W. Musser and Joseph L. Price, 104–105. Nashville: Abingdon, 2003.

Kiley, Frederick and J.M. Shuttleworth, eds. *Satire: From Aesop to Buchwald*. Indianapolis: Bobbs-Merrill, 1971.

Lewis, C.S. *The Lion, the Witch and the Wardrobe*. New York: HarperCollins, 2000.

———. *The Screwtape Letters*. New York: Bantam, 1982.

Martin, R.A. "Humor." In *Baker Encyclopedia of Psychology*, edited by David G. Benner, 540. Grand Rapids: Baker, 1985.

Milnes, Richard Moncton. "Memoir of the Author." In *The Poetical Works of Thomas Hood, Volume 1*, xii. New York: James Miller, 1867.

Rabelais, Francois. *The Histories of Gargantua and Pantagruel*. In *The Portable Rabelais*, selected, translated, and edited by Samuel Putnam, 187. New York: Viking, 1968.

Ryken, Leland et al., eds. "Humor." In *Dictionary of Biblical Imagery*, 409. Downers Grove, IL: InterVarsity, 1998.

Sanders, Barry. *Sudden Glory: Laughter as Subversive History*. Boston: Beacon, 1995.

Scott, R.B.Y. *The Relevance of the Prophets, Revised Edition*. New York: Macmillan, 1976.

Therese, de Lisieux, Saint. *Story of a Soul: The Autobiography of St. Therese of Lisieux*. Translated by John Clarke. Washington, DC: ICS Publications, 1976.

Trueblood, Elton. *The Humor of Christ*. New York: Harper & Row, 1975.

www.ingramcontent.com/pod-product-compliance
Lightning Source LLC
Chambersburg PA
CBHW071105090426
42737CB00013B/2497